The Adventurous Journey

A Family Following God

Dan Kellogg

Printed in the United States of America

ISBN 978-0-9966409-0-9

Editor: Kira Hagenbuch Monica/Dawn Shell/Kami Moore
Cover Designer: Adrian Sims

Unless noted, all quoted Scripture from New Living Translation, Tyndale House Publishers

Dedication

This book is dedicated to my wife, Audrey, who has chosen to adventure with me since June 3rd, 1978. She has trusted me to lead her to more places than she wanted to go. She has been my companion and friend through it all. I know that we will have many more adventures together.

Without you, Audrey, my adventures don't have the same meaning. Thank you for adventuring with me as we follow God.

Contents

Foreword

Some of the oldest and most widespread stories in the world are stories of adventure. Adventures are exciting or unusual experiences that can take us to faraway places, or just far out of our comfort zone. Often times, they are potentially fraught with risky undertakings and uncertain outcomes. More often than not, adventure can change us and change our perspective on life. The experiences we have while on an adventure allow our spirit and the wild side of our hearts to grow.

By the time Dan and Audrey came into my life, their children were grown and they had recently become empty nesters. Having had the adventure of a lifetime together raising a family, they now had their sights on new adventures that would take us to places I hadn't imagined of going. Without their thirst to seek out new quests, I would never have made it to the summit of Mt. Kilimanjaro and seen the world from the top of Africa. Only to return with them two years later to take on a new challenge of hunting big game in the wilds of Namibia. To the north we've adventured on the skirts of the Yukon territories chasing moose from dawn until dusk, and we've had amazing experiences in Mexico helping our brothers and sisters to the south build a new church in an area where hope only comes in fits and starts. All of these adventures have changed me in that my horizons are wider than before and my thirst to see more of God's creation and all of his different peoples is now unquenchable.

In this book, Dan and Audrey set out to share their adventures of raising a family, in the midst of starting a church, which has become one of the biggest in the Northwest. While their story may not be the same as yours, I believe their life experiences in raising kids are much the same as most of us encounter on this journey. My wife and I have come to rely on the wisdom that hindsight has given Dan and Audrey so that we may learn from their successes, and failures. Who knows, by reading the pages that lay ahead, you just might find an adventure to relate to as well that will help you understand and communicate to your family in a new way.

Dominique Ruybal
Friend and fellow adventurer for life

Introduction

I nervously watched a redhead move across the lunchroom at our college campus. She caught my eye. She was full of life, so I went and sat down across from her and her boyfriend. He was a tall skinny dude with a mustache. When he turned sideways, he could be mistaken for a broom. As Audrey describes it, "Dan sat at the table and instantly the excitement and electricity of his personality changed the whole atmosphere. He began his pursuit and persistence of me, just as every girl dreams." The guy she was dating was more than kind to allow me to join them in the cafeteria, library, or walking wherever. But I would totally take over the conversation. For the next few days we ate together and walked to class together - just the three of us. Finally, I made my move. I invited her rabbit hunting. There's nothing more romantic than a hike in the woods that ends with barbecued rabbit. *Would she go? Could she shoot? Did she like adventure?* This was my first test to see if she was The One.

The Adventure Begins

Starting a family is an adventure for anyone. We all have our stories - or we will have a story. This book is about that adventure. That adventure can be done correctly - or it can end up in disaster. Half the families today end up failing. In this book, my wife Audrey and I will share from our adventures. We have done some things right, and we hope you will learn from our successes. We have also done some things wrong. We hope you will also learn from our failures. Along with our story, we will look at the story of

Abraham and Sarah in the Bible. We will see and learn from their successes and failures, too. Their adventure is recorded in Genesis. Abram became Abraham, the father of faith. In the New Testament we discover he has the faith we need for the promise of God's adventurous plan for our own families.

> *Therefore, the promise comes by faith, so that it may be by grace and may be guaranteed to all Abram's offspring…also to those who have the faith of Abram. He is the father of us all. (Romans 4:16)*
>
> *Against all hope, Abram in hope believed and so became the father of many nations, just as it had been said to him, "So shall your offspring be." (Romans 4:18)*
>
> *So also Abram "believed God, and it was credited to him as righteousness."*
> *Understand, then, that those who have faith are children of Abram. Scripture foresaw that God would justify the Gentiles by faith, and announced the gospel in advance to Abram: "All nations will be blessed through you."*
> *So those who rely on faith are blessed along with Abram, the man of faith. (Galatians 3:6-9)*

As you read this book you will be introduced to our faith and to the faith of Abraham. Faith in our Creator changes everything. It especially helps us when we fail. This kind of faith gives us the courage to give grace to those family members who may fail us along the way. We will learn how to travel a path of faith from others' successes and failures.

Chapter 1

False Start

It was 5th grade, around springtime. Something was stirring in my soul and in my class. Girls began to catch my eye and there was a constant drama beginning to happen in our class. Kids were "going together" - becoming couples. Some of the boys and girls were actually talking to each other or, unbelievably, holding hands. I entered into the fray one day by mentioning to one of my friends that I was interested in a girl named Dana. I watched and waited for the courage to do something about it. Finally, I spent some hard-earned cash (about a dollar) on a beautiful ring. I wrote a note asking her to go with me. I carefully folded it with the ring inside and sent it across the room to her. By now the whole room was in on the drama. The only exception was the teacher. I watched as Dana wrote her response and sent it back to me. I carefully opened it…the message was clear: "No way!" My first attempt at love was crushed.

Maybe your attempts to start your family adventure were as successful as mine. Abraham and Sarah also had a false start. We know that Terah, Abraham's father, was the original adventurer. We are not told, so we can only guess how his journey started. Terah had the terrible loss of a son named Haran and we don't know anything of his wife. We just know that he started off to the land of Canaan.

> *Terah took his son Abram, his grandson Lot son of Haran, and his daughter-in-law Sarai, the wife of his son Abram, and together they set out from Ur of the Chaldeans to go to Canaan. But when they came to Harran, they settled there. (Genesis 11:31)*

We do not know why they started for the land of Canaan, but we know they started on an adventure only to stop short. They left the town of Ur and headed northwest, to go around the desert. When they got about halfway to the town of Harran, they stopped. We don't know how long they stopped, but we know they failed to move on. Their adventure stalled right at the halfway point. It is easy to stop halfway. It is easy to get weary. It is easy to start but hard to keep going.

For some of you, right up front I want to acknowledge that you may have faced rejection and failure. Your journey has stopped way short of what you planned. For some of you, the thought of family only brings painful memories. And then for some of you, you are thinking about stopping your adventure. It is just too hard. It is not what you thought it would be. If this is you and you are in this difficult place, do not stay there: let God help you move past your pain and failures. Start again on a great adventure.

I am glad for the next chapter in my life. The real adventure begins. I am glad for **your** next chapter. I can't wait to hear your story.

Chapter 2

Initial Testing

It was a sunny fall afternoon, a beautiful day for a date. I think it was our second date. The birds sang in the trees and the red squirrels gathered nuts. It was warm, with a slight breeze, as we started into the woods. We were deep in the woods; the oak trees provided an amazing canopy. We snuggled in next to one of the trees to get to know each other. Neither of us was saying a word, the only sound was the rustle of the leaves and the wind. Then it happened - Bam! We bagged our dinner — a squirrel hit the deck. The next thing I knew we were both elbow deep in squirrel guts. I could not ask for a better test. Audrey stayed right with me, and to my dismay, often outshot me. The conversation at dinner was rich because of the adventure in the afternoon. She was passing my test. The question soon hit me: *Would I pass her test*? This would be tricky because there are not too many who would put up with the adventure I believed God had for us.

The story of how Abraham and Sarah got married was never written down. As I understand it, their marriage was arranged. They would have been very young. The parents got to select the best partner for each child. Who better to know what each child needs? Whoever made the choice made a good one because Sarah agreed to go on a lifelong faith adventure that would change our world.

We all have the choice today. Our marriages are the result of our selections. We all have a story or will have a story of how things began. I think sometimes we don't test each candidate the way we should. So, if you are still dating, here is my story and the test I put my wife through. You will get her story too, but don't believe everything she says.

I wanted someone who would adventure with me to the unknown.

I knew that our lives would be an adventure. I planned to live my life on a mission field in South America. I wanted someone who would follow me into the unknown. There is no better test than a hike - or even better, camping. Camping sometimes provides some serious hardship, and often times it's my fault. I had to ask the question "*Would she be fun to be with in camp?*" I have spent way too many camping trips with someone in the camp who no one wanted to be around. I needed to see what would happen when things didn't go quite right (which is the case on most of my trips). If the only time we see our potential spouse is under perfect circumstances, we'll never know what they are made of. I had a few girlfriends who never made it past the first requirements. I asked one girlfriend if she would travel with me to foreign countries and have kids in foreign hospitals. She said "no" and was gone. Audrey is a tough girl. She passed with flying colors.

I wanted someone who could hunt.

I love to hunt. I spend hours preparing for hunting. I spend hours looking at things in the store that could help me hunt. I spend days and weeks on hunting trips. Hunting is the one thing that restores my soul. I love to be in the outdoors and hunting puts me there at all hours of the day and night. The adventure of hunting is really the adventure of the unknown. I enjoy eating healthy, wild meat that also brings back memories and stories of those trips. I respect people who don't hunt and don't eat wild game, but I wanted a woman who could outshoot, outhunt, and outlast most people. If you can't enjoy recreation together you will miss out on a huge part of life.

I wanted someone who loved God.

At age twelve I knew God wanted me to be in ministry. I never wavered from that call. My future spouse could limit my future ministry. Ministry is a hard job. I felt called to it and would not compromise. I knew that ministry would lead me to tough places. Jesus led His disciples to the cross. I needed a partner who would love God more than me. When she put God first in her life and I put God first in my life the Union would become one force following Him. Some people say they love God; I wanted someone who *lived* like they loved God. Audrey and I spent three days fasting and asking God about our future relationship. We asked for His leadership before we asked each other to commit for life. If you are in the process of deciding if the person loves God, here are a couple of good tests:

You can tell they love God by how they spend their time.

If they love God they will begin their week with Him. They will make time for worship. God loves the church - it is His bride. She will love the church, too. If she loves God she will begin her day with God, talking to Him and listening to Him. If she loves God she will be in service to Him. Her time will be given doing things for God.

You can tell they love God by how they spend their money.

If she loves God she will put him first in her finances. Ten percent is a minimum. The generous spirit that comes from a heart focused on God is what you are after. If money has a hold on a potential partner, you will fight this all your lives. Here is a good question: Does she honor God with her tithe even when she can't afford to? One time Audrey and I gave away our old car to missions. We couldn't afford to do it, but felt like God wanted us to. In the early days of ministry we learned that God takes care of those who generously give.

Audrey's Tests

Those godly standards were hard to meet. I left many behind on the way to finding the right partner. The moment Audrey and I began to spend time together, I realized she was The One. But Audrey had dated several times and each relationship had left her feeling void of anything that seemed right so she made a promise to God to wait for the right one. As she tells it "I was going to put my faith to the test, trust God, and I was NOT going to get into a relationship with anyone unless I knew that was what God wanted. This was a big step for me." It took four months for me to pass her tests, before I stole the first kiss. That is right - we did not kiss for four months. "I was not even going to kiss Dan or allow him to kiss me, still holding strong to my promise to God," Audrey says. It finally happened in the car. We slowly drove on a back street when I suggested she kiss my cheek. She went for it - and I turned my head.

Even though Audrey was falling head over heels, I had to pass her test. She felt impressed to fast and pray during lunch for five days, so she asked that we not see each other during that time but she did not tell me why. I prayed for her and fasted for her, asking that God would help her through whatever hardship she was going through. I told her roommate one day to let her know I was doing this and thinking about her. This was the sign she was waiting for. The fact that I was praying and fasting simultaneously without her knowing it was the sign that she needed from God to stay in this relationship, it was God's will at this time.

My advice to those who are still looking, don't compromise your standard. Focus on the inside beauty that will last. Every day my wife gets more beautiful because of her heart. The longer you spend time together, the more you understand that beauty is way deeper than your skin. I am amazed at what surgeons can do to change the outside these days. But only God can remove the ugliness of the human soul. Only God can create a new person. Only God can fill a heart with love that is so attractive that the outside begins to reflect the inside in a way that reveals real beauty. That is worth investing in.

My advice to those who didn't take the time to get it right: let God make things right. The story of Abraham and Sarah is for you. We don't get the early part of their marriage or their family history, but it must not have been good. Two teenagers being put together without a choice in the matter couldn't have been easy. The lessons of marriage are hard but even harder for teenagers. God called them out of their past and gave them a future. They made a lot of mistakes on the way, but it was a promise of blessings that kept them moving forward. God wants to bless your family. God wants to help you.

Chapter 3

Dream of Adventure

I fitted one of my heavy old packs to Audrey's back because I couldn't afford the latest gear. We were about to take our first camping trip in the Cascade Mountain Range together. We had just moved back to Washington to begin our ministry. We had been married for fourteen years and our kids were at ages that they really didn't need us around as much. So we left on a trip together. Her pack was heavy (she says it was fifty pounds, but I beg to differ). She never complained but I could sense her fear of the unknown. She was following me to a place I had never been before. It was a place with two little lakes I had seen on a map. There wasn't a trail to them, so we would make our own. I am not sure I should have chosen this as the first hike, but it stirred my soul. Other lakes would have a clear trail and crowds, but our little lakes would provide solitude. Who else would dare to blaze their own trail? I was excited and Audrey was nervous when we locked the car and headed off up a steep hillside. The day was warm and sunny; the hillside was a little slick from the dew of the morning. I would soon learn that I had to teach Audrey to trust her boots. I also needed to learn to pace myself and make this enjoyable for her.

After a few hours of climbing, we arrived way above the lakes. To my great pleasure we could actually see the lakes. There were two routes to the lake we would be camping beside. One was a direct route down a steep cliff-like embankment. It was about 500 feet down and then up the other side. I like the direct route, so off we went. Only a few yards down, I was in trouble. My wife was scared. It was steep, and I mean **steep**. I have hiked a lot and know the limits of my abilities. This was steep but doable for me. I realized that she had never been on such a steep slope. If she didn't trust her boots and suddenly sat down out of fear, she would begin to slide and then tumble. I would see her at the bottom of the ravine and this idea of a lifetime of camping would be over - and maybe our lives too. I did my best to coach her past the danger but she froze and refused to go farther. We spent the next hour getting off this cliff. She told me that if she ever made it out, she wouldn't hike with me again. When we finally arrived at the top again we took the second route. By skirting the hill we would have a much more gradual descent into the lakes.

When we traveled around we discovered someone had made a trail…a wide easy trail. I had to ask a serious question about my leadership. *Why would I choose the hard trail?* That is a question I still get asked from time to time. When I think about the question it seems obvious to me. We all need to test our limits. When we do something really hard, everything else seems easy. The more hard things I do, the easier life seems to me. We arrived at our first overnight camp. Besides the fear of bears and mountain lions, the trip was a huge success. Through it all, even though she vowed to never hike with me again, she learned to never say never! We have been adventuring together ever since. And yes, she occasionally adjusts my route as we travel.

Sometimes God asks us to follow Him through hard places, too. He certainly did that with Abraham and Sarah. Their story is an amazing adventure. I can't imagine what it was like for Abraham and Sarah when God called them. Listen to what God says to them.

> *The LORD had said to Abram, "Leave your native country, your relatives, and your father's family, and go to the land that I will show you." (Genesis 12:1)*

I think God wanted to move them away from the influences of others that had no faith. Leave everything behind… your house, your friends, your family, your security. God calls them to a great adventure. He calls every one of us to an adventure but we can only follow God fully when we let go of everything that would hold us back.

Sometimes the customs of our native country are not how God wants to build our marriage. He wanted to start something new and in order to do this Abraham and Sarah would have to let go of everything they knew.

Sometimes our friends draw us away from our adventure. You can see your future by the friends you hang out with. Take a close look at the lifestyle of your friends - you are either influencing them or they are influencing you.

Sometimes our families can get in the way. Your lifetime story must begin with following God. Sometimes He knows you have to let go of your family to create something new. I can't imagine how the conversation went with Abraham and Sarah and their parents. If our kids come to us describing an adventure, I hope we will be ready to let go and let God lead them. The faith adventure always begins by letting go. Here is why they were willing to let go.

> *I will make you into a great nation. I will bless you and make you famous, and you will be a blessing to others. (Genesis 12:2)*

"I will bless you and make you famous." Wow, what a promise! Hang on to the dream that God has given you. Abraham and Sarah were to be blessed to become a blessing to everyone in the world. They did not have kids. They had no future, but they had faith in God that He would make them into a family that would change the world.

This promise is for us, too. He has promised to bless us. God calls us to become a family that is a blessing.

My grandpa set the standard for our family. He decided to live his life and teach his kids to be a blessing. As a family, Grandma and Grandpa started three churches and ran three church camps. All while they ran a successful business. Their kids became powerful ministers. One traveled to Africa as a missionary to Kenya. One traveled the country as an evangelist that worked with churches and camps. One became a strong businessman that funded ministry and helped churches everywhere that he went. God has a dream for your family. We need to hang on to that dream. He will bless us to be a blessing. I am grateful today that the adventure God has called our family to is one of blessing. Both of our kids are in ministry. They arrange their lives in such a way that they are a blessing to everyone who knows them. I hang on to the dream that God has for our family.

There came a time for Abraham and Sarah to actually set out and here is what happened.

> *After that, Abram traveled south and set up camp in the hill country, with Bethel to the west and Ai to the east. There he built another altar and dedicated it to the LORD, and he worshiped the LORD. (Genesis 12:8)*

For Abraham and Sarah to become a blessing as God promised, they had to believe. The very first thing Abraham did was set up an altar. The altar was at the center of everything they did. They would offer sacrifices on this altar. Everyone who traveled with Abraham would discover what was important to him. When Abraham traveled to a new place there was always a list of things to do, but the first thing on the list was a place of worship. Our faith in God must rise to the top in everything we do.

The second thing Abraham did was worship. When Genesis says he worshiped God, I wonder what happened. I wonder what he felt. I know that he would have sacrificed animals, but I wonder if something more happened in his heart. More than once while on my adventures I have been overwhelmed with the presence of God. I remember after one long week of elk hunting, I had hiked well over a hundred miles without seeing one elk. It didn't matter - I was enjoying God's creation. With just a few hours to go on the last hike, on the way back to the cabin, I mentioned to God how nice some elk meat would be. As I neared the cabin, a bull elk ran in front of me fifteen yards away. I harvested the elk that day but more importantly, I worshiped God. I wept in His presence. I knew that God cared about me. I knew that God was my provider. I also knew that God didn't always give me game when I suggested it, but I always seem to find Him on my adventures. He is where I put my faith.

Chapter 4

Temptation and Struggles

It was early in the morning the first day of our caribou hunt. We woke up from a restless night. Water was frozen in a pan. It was starting to drizzle. Audrey and I were camping with my brother Ron and we had invited our old wrestling coach Tom Black to travel with us. We had been dropped off by floatplane after traveling from Bethel, Alaska to somewhere in the tundra. The plane had flown in over the lake where we were going to stay. I suggested a spot near the end of the lake. As we neared this spot, a grizzly stood up and took a swipe at the plane. Audrey's thought: "What was I thinking doing this?"

Needless to say, we changed our spot. As we set up camp, we spotted the grizzly on the hill above our lake. It was a huge boar (male), which is why we didn't sleep too well that night. We hurriedly fixed breakfast in our makeshift kitchen set up on big clumps of tundra. We had two bags of oatmeal and some coffee and it would have to last us until lunch. Our coach was better supplied. His food consisted of oatmeal, eggs, muffins and candy bars. It did give us some sense of comfort to think that his food supply would be much more appetizing to a bear. There were no trees to hang our food in, so we hoped for the best.

We hiked up the hill to a lookout spot. Just after we sat down, Audrey spotted a grizzly bear less than two hundred yards away. It got our attention. Then we saw a herd of caribou running away from us. They looked like trophies, so my brother and I just took off running. We were in full pursuit with nothing else on our minds. It did not occur to me that I had just left my wife and coach behind at the last spot we had seen the grizzly. One thing I noticed very quickly, no matter how fast you run, you will never catch a caribou. I realized I had left them behind chasing something I could never catch.

I am pretty sure there are many of us that make the mistake of chasing after things while leaving our loved ones behind. It seems like you come to your senses and realize that it wasn't worth it. I was wrong and I needed to admit it. In the following verses Abraham left his wife behind. It was wrong - and it wasn't worth it.

> *Now there was a famine in the land, and Abram went down to Egypt to live there for a while because the famine was severe. As he was about to enter Egypt, he said to his wife Sarai, "I know what a beautiful woman you are. When the Egyptians see you, they will say, 'This is his wife. Let's kill him; then we can have her!' (Genesis 12:10-12)*

Our imaginations play all kinds of games with us. When on an adventure called marriage, we can let our imagination talk us into all kinds of mistakes. In this passage, we see Abraham was all about saving his own skin. He was all about his problems. When we get into this mode we are in trouble. We will do the wrong thing.

One of my early mistakes in our marriage was getting angry at Audrey on a public street in Iowa. It was in the little town of Oskaloosa and I was the new youth minister in town. We were on a tight budget. We bought our first house, were having a child, and both of us were finishing college without incurring any debt. It was early in our marriage and we were having a blast together. We were great friends. One day we disagreed on how to spend what little money we had. While Audrey doesn't remember the details of the fight, she does remember my anger over the amount of money. "Our budget was twenty dollars. I wrote a check for $20.10," she says. When Audrey didn't see where I was coming from, I decided that if I yelled at her she would finally understand. I yelled and she got quiet. I could feel the chill in the air immediately. In my effort to bully my friend into getting things my way I left her behind and damaged our relationship.

I had some growing up to do. I had to learn how to control my anger. I had to learn that anger is the emotion that makes you feel in control when you are actually out of control. I know why Jesus' brother James said: *"the anger of man never produces the righteousness of God."*

That anger issue doesn't stop with your spouse. When you add a child to the mix everything changes. Kids quickly learn how to push our buttons. If we are not careful we will give our kids the experience of living with angry parents. The anger meant to control never works like we want it to. Discipline out of anger may temporarily change behavior but it damages the heart. Arguments full of anger may give you a win, but never the change you really desire. Our anger is always the red light on the dashboard of our soul. It tells you there is something wrong. It tells you it is time to seek help. It tells you that you have a problem. I know you will say "But I had my reasons for getting angry." Opening yourself up to an honest question from those who love you most will be revealing. Ask "Do I get angry too often?" No excuses now. If the answer is "yes" it's time to admit your issue and make some changes. You can tell the maturity of a person by the ability to gain control of their anger. Alcohol and anger often go together because an alcoholic quits maturing the moment the alcohol takes control.

Back to Abraham… he was trying to save his own skin so what would he do?

> *"So please tell them you are my sister. Then they will spare my life and treat me well because of their interest in you."(Genesis 12:13)*

Tell them you are my sister? Ouch… makes me feel better for a moment about my mistakes. Think about it. In his mistake, he is about to throw away God's dream for his family. If the Pharaoh sleeps with her and she gives birth, the story that God intended would never have happened. I am so glad God intervened.

There are moments of temptation that will come to every family. The easy way is to give in. The easy way is to believe a lie. Even while reading this, some people will be playing with temptations that can damage their family.

What was Abraham's temptation? He knew that Sarah looked good (stunning apparently). He knew that the outside looks of Sarah could be sold to give him a seemingly more secure and better standing in the country.

Our culture begs us to sell ourselves for the attraction of the outside. God created men to be enticed by the beauty of women. Or some would say, God created women to entice men with their beauty. It is probably both. Women often play with that power. That attraction can be misused. In our culture it is called plastic surgery, Botox, pornography, prostitution or anything that simply reduces a person into an object. Don't get me wrong, I am amazed at the way surgeons can make us look better than we do. The bigger issue is why are you doing it? Do you need this? If we are not careful we can end up selling our soul for something that is only skin deep.

Some people will be tempted to spice up their marriage or personal life with pornography, only to find that it can ruin the dream of the healthy family that God had in mind for them. Do your research and you will find that in the long term those things never give you what you want. Studies are easily available online at covenanteyes.com, pornharmsresearch.com, and pinkelephantresources.com. All of these sites teach the same thing: pornography kills the greatest gift that God gave a couple. If you need to develop a healthy sex life, get educated and discover what researchers are now confirming: pornography ruins the sex life as found in long-term, healthy monogamous marriages ("What Porn Does to Intimacy" published by P. Streep 2014).

Because of work situations, we are put in close working relationships with the opposite sex. This affords us the ability to play with temptation. We develop close relationships with the opposite sex that begin to cross the line. If your confidant is a person of the opposite sex, you are in the danger zone. You will begin to share more than you should, and before too long, you will end up regretting it. If you play with temptation and you are not careful, you can throw away the dream. Relationships that begin with an adulterous affair almost always fail. The start of any relationship by cheating creates a very insecure future. I have talked with some that have somehow endured and their relationship is one of distrust and guilt. One man asked me to share these words with anyone who would listen. "It isn't worth it. Do what it takes to work on your relationship, but don't fall for this trap. Don't leave your spouse behind."

Sometimes the affair is not with a person, it is with a drug like alcohol, prescription drugs or any addictive drug. Without meaning to, you get caught in a dangerous cycle. It is just as damaging. Your choice to return to your love requires a willingness to seek help. Thankfully I have seen many families return to health after the choice to enter drug treatment or drug counseling. Don't leave your spouse behind.

For some, the affair is with food. This is a hidden danger in our families today. If we make unhealthy choices with food we will make unhealthy choices with our family. This is not a focus on body size or body image; this is a focus on health. We have a responsibility to keep our health. If food becomes our master we leave our family behind, or take them down a dangerous path with us.

Sometimes the affair is with work. Your real love is your job, not your family. You find more success and more affirmation at work than you do at home, so you just leave your family behind. This is one of the mistakes I made in our adventure. I used all of my creativity on my job. I found all my affirmation at work and not at home. I left no creative energy for my family or my marriage. The more I got involved in ministry the more I realized I could help people with their marriages and their families. During almost every meal I had with my family, I was called away to help someone. My wife and kids sacrificed family time so I could help others. At the end of the day, I came home to a family that still needed me and I had nothing left for them. I made some changes at work for my marriage and my family - that saved me from disaster. I made a concerted effort to take a day off and creatively spend time with the family. In order to protect that day, I scheduled time for them so that they knew they could count on me. For my marriage, I committed to a date night that was scheduled and nothing could displace that. I slowly learned that if Audrey was going to be with me in my old age, I couldn't leave her behind. We never hear Sarah complain about Abraham's bad idea. I have never really heard Audrey complain, but our relationship is so much better when we travel together.

Chapter 5

Choices

It was 1978. Audrey and I had only been married for six months and our adventurous life was in full swing. She was three months pregnant and finishing her senior year of college at Vennard. I was still a junior at William Penn in Iowa working full time and going to college full time. We had bought our first house together. I had just started my first ministry job as a youth minister. At age twenty, I was in charge of about 150 kids. Our budget was tight. We were learning to make it on our own. We did not believe in debt for college so we were paying for school out of our living expenses. We lived on a very limited budget. We had nothing, but had everything. We tithed $19 of our $190 a week salary. Our meat came from rabbits (the limit was twenty a day) and squirrels I could shoot, and our vegetables came from our garden. We were stretched to the max!

It was then that our church made a big push to help out our brothers and sisters in Guatemala. We had nothing to give but we felt like God wanted us to do something, even though we were already doing the impossible with very little. Obedience to God's spirit is sometimes counter to our checkbook. We couldn't afford it! How could we have faith to give what we didn't have? Abraham's faith would teach us that lesson. The next chapter in Abraham and Sarah's life is one of learning to give generously – and even giving until it hurts.

As we pick up the story, things were going really well for Abraham and his nephew Lot.

> *Lot, who was traveling with Abram, had also become very wealthy with flocks of sheep and goats, herds of cattle, and many tents. But the land could not support both Abram and Lot with all their flocks and herds living so close together. So disputes broke out between the herdsmen of Abram and Lot. (At that time Canaanites and Perizzites were also living in the land.) (Genesis 13:5-7)*

One thing I have learned about family life is that you will eventually fight about money. Many couples will have their biggest fights about money. One person always wants to hang on to every penny and another wants to spend every penny. Someone will want to have more and it will never be enough, while the other will be satisfied. The conflicts of what we do with money will make us better partners or split us apart. We have a choice regarding how we move forward with our finances. The choices you are going to read about below were ones that defined two families, and their choices set them to go in very different directions.

> *Finally Abram said to Lot, "Let's not allow this conflict to come between us or our herdsmen. After all, we are close relatives! The whole countryside is open to you. Take your choice of any section of the land you want, and we will separate." (Genesis 13:8-9)*

Lot chose the cities of Sodom and Gomorrah. The pastures were rich and the cities provided a permanent place to settle. No more living in a tent. But the cities were corrupt and scheduled for destruction. His choice to live in the city would cost him his wife, most of his family and all his wealth.

Two angels came to rescue Lot and his family because of a conversation Abraham had with God (Genesis 18). But Lot's family was reluctant to leave. Even after leaving, the lure of the wealth and luxury of the city made his wife look back longingly, which was the one thing the angels warned them not to do. She instantly became a pillar of salt and ended up dead along with the rest of the citizens that lived in the excess of these cities. His own sons never left the city. They were unwilling to give up their wealth to follow God. Only Lot and two daughters were left. All his wealth and most of his family perished in the fire. This was the result of the choice Lot made when he picked the rich land of Sodom and Gomorrah.

Even though Abraham had every right to the best land, he gave away the wealth of the best pastures. The humility and generosity of Abraham is unbelievable. I wonder what Sarah thought about his decision. I wonder if they talked it through. That was a defining moment for Abraham. His act of humility and generosity moved him away from Sodom and Gomorrah. It brought him to a new level of faith. Could he survive with less? He had been very blessed by God. His faith was rewarded in unbelievable ways. Every day his wealth of cattle had grown. What would this decision do for his wealth?

The choices we make with our finances will set the direction for our family. I am reminded that all our wealth will perish in the fire. Only what we give remains with us. When our church made that commitment to help Guatemalans, Audrey and I were challenged to give by faith. We had one car, a 1967 Barracuda that was damaged on one side from a wreck. We put it up for sale and gave all $700 from the sale of it to the mission offering. We trusted that somehow God would provide. We both felt like it was what God wanted. It was an adventure in generosity. It was crazy faith.

Our gift of $700 came back to us in an amazing way. The church paid our way on the thirty-day mission trip to Guatemala that we, ourselves, couldn't afford. It was a lesson in God's provision. It was our first Christmas together and the first Christmas either of us had spent away from home. We traveled to Guatemala just two years after a major earthquake had devastated the city. We still felt aftershocks every day when we were there building a training center for pastors. I knew nothing about construction, but I learned to lay brick and pour concrete while on that trip. Our little Barracuda was part of all of this. We could not afford to give, but by faith we were experiencing the joy of our first adventure as a married couple we could have never afforded. God has amazing ways of rewarding generosity.

Our unity as a couple was strengthened by the miracles we were seeing and living through together. Audrey now says that she cannot remember a time when she was sad about not being able to buy things she wanted or wished to have. "God was so faithful. To live and experience how God would provide for us was the richest blessing and evidence of His faithfulness. It's something anyone can experience." Obedience and generosity gave us a surprise adventure. The memory of our first Christmas together is a reminder of where God led us.

The story of Abraham's faith in generosity sets a couple benchmarks for us, one of the heart and one of finances. If you look closely at his choices you will see obedience and generosity. After winning a great victory and bringing home more wealth than he could have imagined, he made another choice of faith.

> *After Abram returned from his victory over Kedorlaomer and all his allies, the king of Sodom*

went out to meet him in the valley of Shaveh (that is, the King's Valley). And Melchizedek, the king of Salem and a priest of God Most High, brought Abram some bread and wine. Melchizedek blessed Abram with this blessing: "Blessed be Abram by God Most High, Creator of heaven and earth. And blessed be God Most High, who has defeated your enemies for you." Then Abram gave Melchizedek a ***tenth*** *of all the goods he had recovered. (Genesis 14:17-20)*

The choice to give a tenth (a tithe) involved both obedience and generosity. Melchizedek represented God and God's work. Abraham had asked God if he should go and rescue his nephew from an army that had raided his village. God gave him a promise and a victory. Now he was returning with all the wealth of the defeated army. He believed everything he had was from God. He also knew that God wanted him to keep 90% of it. So he honored God with 10%. This clear decision to tithe was an act of worship. Melchizedek did not ask for the money, but Abraham gave the 10% (tithe).

Audrey and I learned early in our lives that we had to tithe. When we gave, amazing things happened, just like when we sold the Barracuda. Somehow God made our giving stretch beyond what we knew it could. What we discovered was that we couldn't afford not to tithe. Our tithe set in motion for us a blessing we could not anticipate. The decision to trust God by giving Him 10% of our wealth changed us and made us better people.

The step to tithe will start you on the biggest adventure of your life. There is always an excuse to not tithe. I am sure there is someone in your family right now that does not want to tithe. But I can tell you, and Abraham has shown us, that the choices you make with your money will determine the direction of your adventure. Will you give and discover what God has for you? Or will you choose a life that will eventually burn up in the fire? If Lot could have somehow seen the future, he would have chosen generosity. It is time to choose and see where God will lead you.

We have never out-given God. At times we have given all our savings. In obedience we have given our life insurance policy. We have sold our house three times to help in our building campaign. Today we are rich in all of the adventures He has given us. We can't wait for the next adventure. We know we are not done trusting Him. We are learning every day that a choice to give generously is a choice for adventure.

Chapter 6

Facing Your Fears

It was the middle of the night, about one a.m., and the alarm was going off. The temperature was around zero degrees Fahrenheit. At 15,500 feet, the air was so thin that we would wake up gasping for air at night. There was no moon so it was pitch black out. The only thing we could see were the head lamps piercing the darkness. We were told that one of our crew members was sick…really sick. We had already lost two porters (porters carry your camp gear, food and water and they are required on Kilimanjaro) to altitude sickness and now this woman from our crew would have to turn back as well. Cerebral edema had set in and her brain had swollen, causing her to throw up uncontrollably. In a few hours she would be helped down to a lower altitude before her sickness became lethal. This was especially scary because she was the fastest climber and the most prepared among us. Her husband chose to stay with her and help her down the mountain. His bid to the summit was over as well.

Our little band started out into the dark, moonless night right after a cup of coffee and a piece of toast. Deep in our gut we had some lingering fear. We had done all we could to prepare for that moment, but we had a lot of questions. *Would we be able to make it? Could we survive it? Would someone else get hurt?* People still die on this mountain and only half of the people that attempt to summit actually summit Kilimanjaro. Many who were better prepared and better equipped than we were had turned back. *Would I be one who made it? Or would I be one who turned back? Would Audrey make it with me? Or go on without me? Or I without her?*

We traveled in half steps measured out by our guide. We were making our way up the final few miles. In less than two miles, we would scramble up 4,400 feet of elevation gain (from 15,000 to 19,341). It would take six to eight hours of climbing to just reach the rim. Each step was taken in scree (small, round volcanic pebbles). We stepped two feet forward and slid one foot back. Our breathing technique was to inhale deeply and then exhale pursing our lips tightly. With each breath I forced all the air I could into my lungs. The temperature was dropping well below zero and there was a bit of wind rising. All our extremities were feeling the cold. The blood in our bodies was pulling back to the core, leaving us vulnerable to the cold. It was a delicate balance of moving fast enough to stay warm, but not so fast that our bodies would rebel and altitude sickness would take over. It was eerily quiet with only the noise of our shuffling feet.

It was less than an hour into the hike that morning when it hit me. All of the sudden my stomach cramped…I doubled over in pain. I could not go on. I tried in my mind to overcome the pain, but I could not. After all the training and work that went into leading this team to make sure they were ready, it now seemed like my trip was over. I was the one who would not make it. I was unprepared for this moment. My body demanded that I stop and there was nothing I could do.

There are moments just like that for our families. It seems impossible to endure, "I can't go on" moments. Abraham and Sarah had one of those moments. Fear had gripped him. I believe that it suddenly hit him that he was living in a tent in the wilderness with huge amounts of wealth. He was vulnerable for anyone to attack. He had no walls to protect and no way to organize a defense. It would be only a matter of time before someone would take him down. Then God spoke to him.

> *Some time later, the LORD spoke to Abram in a vision and said to him, "Do not be afraid, Abram, for I will protect you, and your reward will be great."*
>
> *And Abram believed the LORD, and the LORD counted him as righteous because of his faith. (Genesis 15:1,6)*

In the dark moments when Abraham experienced fear, he chose to believe in the promise of God; that promise kept him living in a tent. There was the first promise, that one day his family would be a great family that would show the world God exists. His faith in that promise changed everything, yet sleep came hard for him. So God gave him a vision with a new promise, "I will protect you." He believed God. His faith made him stay in a dangerous situation. His faith helped him obey. His faith let him sleep at night.

Abraham believed in two things, blessing and protection. He believed that his God was greater than all the surrounding kings that desired his wealth. He believed that God loved him enough to watch out for him. In that cold dark night, Abraham believed. There must have been many nights full of doubt, but that night was different. Abraham chose faith and God took note.

I have hope that God will help you see His vision for you. He wants you to live a life full of blessings. He wants you to know you are not alone, but that will take faith. You will need faith that God really is watching you; faith that God can take whatever happens to you and make it something good; and faith that God will walk with you through your dark cold nights. Faith in God is a choice and I hope you choose faith for you and your family.

Abraham's faith over fear was reinforced with a covenant from God the next day.

> *After the sun went down and darkness fell, Abram saw a smoking firepot and a flaming torch pass between the halves of the carcasses. So the LORD made a covenant with Abram that day and said, "I have given this land to your descendants, all the way from the border of Egypt to the great Euphrates River." (Genesis 15:17-18)*

This is a graphic picture with the Old Testament sacrifices, but it makes sense to me. God made a promise to Abraham that he and his descendants would live in that land. A promise from the Lord is a covenant, which is a vow until death. God is essentially saying "I will die before I break this promise to you. I will give my life for this covenant." Abraham *chose* to believe in that vow.

On the hillside of Kilimanjaro that night I had a choice to make. Would I go on? I was embarrassed to have to ask the group to stop. I did not want the group to slow down on my behalf. In the pitch black, I stepped off the trail and scrambled down the impossibly steep hill. My body rebelled in horrible ways. My pain was unbearable. After returning to the trail, I told our guide I did not think I could go on. I encouraged Audrey and told her that I wanted her to continue without me. I honestly did not think I would make it to the top.

After discussing it, I made the decision to try and travel as far as I could. I started with ten steps… I made it! So, I went ten more steps… For the next five hours I went ten more steps at a time and I made it to the top *with* my wife! We embraced as we watched the sun come up and the whole world looked different. We were on the top of Africa together because of the faith to go ten more steps.

There have been some dark times in our marriage. They were mostly my failures that put our future in doubt. Those dark times are anchored with a covenant to each other. When we took our vows we did not leave a way out. We said "I would rather die than give up on our covenant." In those dark nights, when you can only see the next step, the future seems impossible. Like that night on the mountain, I looked up ahead a couple times to see how far we had to climb. I saw a string of other climbers' head lamps that seemed to stretch up to the sky. It looked impossible. Only after I looked down to focus on the next ten steps was I able to keep moving.

For Audrey and me, those steps in the dark days of our lives and marriage took us to some good counselors and mentors. We took hard advice from that counsel and made changes that kept us going in the right direction. I learned I could only change myself, so I went about making changes in me. With both of us doing that, we learned to work better together. We intend to see the sunrise together on the top of the universe. We would love to see you there with us. I know you can make it if you choose to believe and take ten more steps.

Chapter 7

Leading through Tough Choices

After fourteen years in ministry I took a year off. I had lost my health and my passion. I had contracted Meniere's disease, which meant that every three days or so I was disabled with terrible dizziness, nausea, and the inability to get out of bed. My passion was waning because I had lost my purpose. I lost the vision God gave me and my balance in life. Audrey had been deeply wounded by the people we served at our church. I knew for her it would be a relief if I would just choose a different career. Hadn't we done enough? Hadn't our sacrifice been enough? Would God allow us to go in a different direction? Only time would answer these questions.

On that year off, I was given an old Arctic Cat snowmobile that had seen better days - it was no longer running. It was just the restoration project I needed, so I began to teach myself to be a snowmobile mechanic. I found a great deal - just $200 on two other "sleds" that were not running. I was able to take all three apart and found enough good parts to build two good sleds. Then, to my good fortune, I found a guy selling a wrecked one for $100. The throttle had stuck and he'd run it into a tree. With a good hammer, I pounded out the front of it. All of the sudden we had three sleds!

I had a makeshift trailer which I loaded with the three sleds, all the tools I could manage, a few bags of extra parts, and we traveled into the mountains. I cringe now at the thought of this. I was not a great mechanic and these were not good machines, but we needed that adventure. We needed the challenge. We needed to do something new.

There was never a trip that we took that didn't involve me working on a sled. In the back of my mind, I was never sure that we would make it back. This fueled the adventure for me. One trip that we took was in the middle of the night. We started a fire and played with the sleds on a steep hill for hours. My aunt had come with her sled as well. It was a great time, but before the night was over we had rolled one sled and my aunt had three broken ribs. Always an adventure!

Each trip into the wilderness began to restore my soul and my health. We still talk about those trips to this day at family gatherings. I learned that broken old sleds can still give you all the adventure you need in life. I am convinced that God held those things together just long enough to restore this broken soul and make me ready for ministry again.

And while I had the snowmobiles to rebuild during this time, God had something else in mind for Audrey to help her through the darkness. She says, "God gave me a special gift in a lady who became my mentor and is still my mentor today. She was the first person to ever look me in the eyes and ask 'How are you doing spiritually?' She has walked with me through all my valleys and mountains, challenged me spiritually, and has been the one I could fully trust. God provided such a unique friendship - the richest gift you could ever ask for is a mentor."

But after that year, the day finally came and I realized that it was time to return to ministry. I knew in my heart there was no other choice. Ministry was a calling I could not shake. I was ready and eager to get back to my passion. Audrey knew it was coming. She did not want to go back, but she knew the covenant we had with our Lord to go and do all the things He wanted us to do. Audrey recalls telling me “I would NEVER go back into ministry” and I said I wouldn’t if she wasn’t with me. She adds, “The weight on my heart became so heavy. I knew that I was keeping him from the very gift God had given him. Then I had an ‘only God’ moment. I saw him come through the doors after a trip to this (the Mill Creek) area, and I knew that I knew. Something happened. And we were headed for ministry. God was so faithful to help us know this is what we were to do.”

This was a leadership challenge. Could I lead our family to a place they did not want to go? Real leadership always has this challenge. In ministry our job is to take people to the cross - to ask people to give up their selfish ways and find new life. Jesus, the greatest leader ever, took his disciples where they didn’t want to go. He took them to the cross.

Abraham was given that challenge as well. One day God decided that His covenant needed a sign…circumcision.

> *This is the covenant that you and your descendants must keep: Each male among you must be circumcised. You must cut off the flesh of your foreskin as a sign of the covenant between Me and you. From generation to generation, every male child must be circumcised on the eighth day after his birth. This applies not only to members of your family but also to the servants born in your household and the foreign-born servants whom you have purchased. All must be circumcised. Your bodies will bear the mark of My everlasting covenant. (Genesis 17:10-13)*

I can only imagine the day Abraham announced to the men in his family that this was going to happen. This was a bad day for many of them! He was leading them somewhere they did not want to go. No choice here. I can only imagine their questions. Who came up with this idea? Why is this so important? Why everybody? If you traveled with Abraham in that day, you sometimes went to hard places and through hard things. This was a painful place.

In our culture today we will sometimes coddle our families. If we are going to be families of faith it is going to cost us. It will be painful at times to follow God. Our willingness to follow is the difference between us and those around us. Our culture wants to set our values. We call for abstinence and the world laughs at us. We tithe while the people in the world spend every dollar on themselves. We set aside worship time, time to serve, and a host of other sacrifices. One day soon, our world will lump us all together as people who hate others. They will take away our tax benefit for giving. This will be the moment we have a choice. Will we follow God even if it costs us everything?

As a pastor, I am continually following God even when it is through a tough place. As I follow Him, I lead others to follow Him as well. I do this because of a calling that has way more rewards than sacrifices. When we lay down everything to follow Him, we win. In the end we are all victorious at the cross. See you there…it is worth it!

Chapter 8

Laughter and Faith

Audrey and I had arrived in the rest camp just before dark. We were in Etosha National Park in Namibia, Africa. We had been lucky to see four lions, a hyena, two rhinos, many elephants and a multitude of plains game from the safety of our rented vehicle that day. We spent hours exploring the National Park, where we were allowed to drive right up to animals and observe them. We were making our way to an open hillside that overlooked a water hole. In the Sahara, every animal has to make a daily trip to the water hole to survive. Each night lions, leopards, and cheetahs came to drink. We sat a few yards away, watching them. There were huge signs that read "Silence is required at the water hole." I assumed the reason for silence was safety. Unlike the other animals, the wild cats could jump the fence and supplement their food supply with slow humans if they wanted. People sat there in silence. Entire families were hardly breathing.

It was a perfect evening: the sun was setting, winds were calm, the temperature was mild, and animals were slowly making their way to the water hole. Audrey wanted to look at pictures from her phone while we waited. As she flipped through the pictures, she hit a video and the volume was as high as it could get. The silence was pierced by the loud, raucous laughter and talking of our friends on the video. I quickly grabbed her phone because she did not know how to stop the video or turn it down. It was blaring and all the people looked at us in disgust. I finally got the volume turned down and the video turned off. She laughed at me because I held the phone and everybody thought I made this huge mistake. I laughed at her laughing at me. We could hardly contain ourselves. Our chuckles had earned us more disdain from the silent crowd all around us. Instead of feeling angry at the situation, this made us laugh.

Finally, we settled back into watching for wildlife and the eyes that had been focused on us were turned to watch for wild cats. There was even a rumor of a pack of wild dogs nearby. Just to be safe, I took my phone out to make sure it was on mute. As I slid the volume controls down, I accidentally hit "play" on the podcast I had been listening to. It was an Easter message and the preacher was excited about the resurrection of Jesus. My phone disrupted the silence –it was even louder than Audrey's! Their eyes were now burning our flesh as they again looked in disgust toward me. This was even funnier to Audrey, who once again could no longer hold in her laughter. We finally just got up and left. We laughed the entire half-mile hike back to our car. It may not have been funny to anyone else, but to us, this was hilarious.

Over the years, laughter has been the medicine for our souls. In her story, Sarah (who was 90, still childless, and according to her own words: "dead") laughed at the notion of being able to have a child. Her 100-year-old husband Abraham was visited by two angels who announced a coming miraculous childbirth.

> *...one of them said, "I will return to you about this time next year, and your wife, Sarah, will have a son!" Sarah was listening to this conversation from the tent. Abraham and Sarah were both very old by this time, and Sarah was long past the age of having children. So she laughed silently to herself and said, "How could a worn-out woman like me enjoy such*

> *pleasure, especially when my master—my husband—is also so old?" (Genesis 18:10-12)*

I like her honesty here. I am old…really old and Abraham was way older… and, well, nothing works like it used to. I wonder if she harkened back to a day when things did work and this made her laugh all the more. I love her laughter. She was not laughing *at* Abraham, she was laughing *with* him. I wonder how much trouble would be averted if we just learned to laugh with each other. Come on, lighten up. When you are facing the impossible in life, laugh at it. It will help you and your relationships. When God asks you to believe in the impossible, laugh at how much you need God to come through for you.

Laughter can be one of the best tools to help your marriage. When times get tougher, laugh a little. When you mess up… laugh more. When you want to yell at each other, just laugh. When you are taking yourself too seriously, get over it and laugh. Your kids need to see you laugh. You *need* to laugh. There are wonderful chemicals released in the brain by simply laughing. This medicine can make life so much easier. Right now, laugh at yourself.

> *Then the LORD said to Abraham, "Why did Sarah laugh? Why did she say, 'Can an old woman like me have a baby?' Is anything too hard for the LORD? I will return about this time next year, and Sarah will have a son." (Genesis 18:13-14)*

In spite of their laughter at having a baby, they believed in God. In spite of the impossibility of a baby in their old age, God came through on their adventure. She became pregnant and named her boy Isaac, which means "he makes me laugh".

Audrey has had to learn to have faith when traveling with me. The experience of visiting Etosha National Park was all a part of a big adventure that took a good deal of convincing. I studied Namibia and Audrey reviewed my plans and finally agreed. As a part of our trip I had discovered an outpost that was hundreds of miles from anywhere. It was in the middle of the Sahara desert. The only way to get there was with a four-wheel drive vehicle. I read the reviews and there was quite a bit of complaining about the roads and the lack of gas stations nearby, but this was a place for a great adventure. We would live with the Bush people and learn their customs. We would hunt alongside them and then learn to make fire and cook what they were able to shoot with their bows. We would hike in the wilderness without guns. We would travel through elephant and lion country looking for any animal that could be fed to their family. Our days and nights would be filled with adventure.

We drove hundreds of miles over dirt roads. At the final government check point (set up to regulate travel through the area) I had noticed the gas gauge was getting lower. I needed it to stay above half a tank to ensure we could make the return trip to the nearest gas station. The roads got smaller and smaller. We traveled up a hill through sandy roads that were steep and narrow. We almost stalled halfway up the hill, but finally made it to the top and to our camp…with the gas gauge on exactly a half a tank. I am not sure I had the faith to believe that a half tank was enough to get us back, but I did not have a choice.

Our stay was amazing! We hunted with the Bushmen and watched as they harvested a large porcupine. We learned to make a fire from the wood without a match. We cooked the whole porcupine on the fire and ate the skin. We danced with the Bush people as they celebrated a successful harvest. We sat around the fire, watching the

Southern Cross in the sky, and laughed together as we told stories.

In the back of my mind, there was an uneasy fear lingering that we would not make our return trip. When it was time to say our goodbyes, we drove away and I mentioned to Audrey that we might have a little problem. I guess I thought it would be good to inform her of our dilemma. With each mile, our gas gauge ticked lower and lower. I tried not to look nervous but it was really going to be close. About halfway back to the nearest station, we were stopped at a checkpoint. The guard asked if we had room for a traveler. I was not prepared for this. It was a pregnant lady and her child. She was a Bush woman. She spoke in clicks (the native language is a series of clicks). I am not much on hitchhikers. I especially did not want someone I did not know. I felt that this was an unreasonable request. It was our vacation, after all. But the guard made us feel obligated and he had a gun. How could we say no? So, good naturedly, we took two hitchhikers on our adventure. We smiled at the child and shared some gum. Things went smoothly. We tried to communicate but we did not do that well, so we ended up traveling in silence.

The dirt road began to get nicer and finally we hit the pavement. There were only thirty miles to go, so I started to feel relief. With just twenty miles left, the car started to sputter. Audrey looked at me to see what was up. Then it suddenly stopped. We realized we were in an impossible situation. How were we supposed to handle this? Should I leave Audrey behind and walk to the station? Do I send her on the road alone? Should we both leave the car with all our belongings and make our way to the station? We were in a no-win situation.

I laughed at our impossible circumstances. Audrey proceeded to apologize to our guests. We had run out of gas. She was stranded with us. This made me laugh all the more. Not only did this woman not understand, she was used to being stranded. It was normal for her. Then an unbelievable thing happened. She pulled out a cell phone and called her friend! Speaking in clicks, she summoned someone to the rescue. Within twenty minutes we had gas and were on our way again.

Is anything too great for God? When you are on His adventure you can be sure He is watching over you and will help you. I do not know how many times Isaac made Abraham and Sarah laugh, but I am guessing laughter made their home a great place. Every impossibility should be met with laughter and faith in a God of the impossible. I wish for every family to have the laughter of Sarah. As Audrey sums up, "Dan will just laugh out loud at the hardships. For us, I understand why he laughs. You can't explain it, you just laugh through it."

Chapter 9

Sex at 100

We had traveled almost eight hours on dirt roads. At one point Audrey thought we were lost. It was a bit further than I had planned. We were tired of looking at the amazing wildlife that Etosha National Park in Namibia, Africa had to offer. Even a lion or a new animal wouldn't interest us enough to slow down or stop. There were very few updated maps and my chosen road was one that had been closed for the last ten years. If I was successful, we would come out at the west end of the park. I just couldn't find the exit, so I had to stop one of the few cars we saw and ask someone for directions. Finally, we made it to our hotel.

I had chosen this hotel because it was close to the Himba tribe, a tribe that has not changed its ways for more than a century; they are nomadic cattle herders. Audrey and I love to see how others live. This would be the second tribe we would spend time with on this adventure. Our hotel was simple: a bed, a shower, and a chair. We stopped to gas up at the nearby store and gas station. While filling the car Audrey noticed a Himba tribal woman entering the store. She was naked from the waist up. It was a little surreal seeing this woman buying her groceries at the local store in her normal attire - or lack thereof.

The next day we visited the tribe and heard their story. It was mostly women who were naked from the waist up. We sat in their mud hut homes. There was a translator to answer our questions. We spent the day learning the Himba ways. We were surprised to learn that they never take baths because water is precious in the desert. That became evident as we stood near them. Their only "bath" was one of smoke. They stood over a fire every day to allow the smoke to drive the bugs away. They would then take fresh hot butter, mix it with red clay, and smear it on their skin. They spent the day taking care of the wealth of their families, cows. It costs a couple of cows to get married and set up your own hut. There were no beds, just mats. Pillows were wood head holders, and only the men were allowed to use those. They subsist on a diet of meat and milk that sits in the sun until it is sour. Families all live in the same hut.

Their lives seemed simple. We learned of the local medicine man that would come around to knock out some teeth of both girls and boys at puberty. Coming of age is painful! It was apparent that sex education was unnecessary. Everyone in the hut would know what was happening. Everyone learned about it the Himba way. I am not in favor of this method, by the way, but it was interesting.

Abraham and Sarah lived in a tent. They became a nomadic tribe, too. Their wealth was also measured in cows. And the Bible says they had sex when they were 100 years old (a miracle moment). Abraham and Sarah's bodies worked again to fulfill God's promise of a child.

> *The LORD kept His word and did for Sarah exactly what He had promised. She became pregnant, and she gave birth to a son for Abraham in his old age. This happened at just the time God had said it would... (Genesis 21:1-3)*

God gave them a son and their lives changed forever.

Sex is fun, even at 100. God created it as a great gift for us. Unlike the Himbas, most of us are uneducated about sex. We may understand the plumbing but not the intense connection that God created in the act of marriage. In a perfect world you will grow up and wait for your wedding night to experience sex. On that night you will begin to connect in a new way. Your sexual fulfillment will release a chemical as addictive as cocaine. Your connection to each other is meant to make you addicted to each other. Jesus quoted Genesis and said "*This explains why a man* ***leaves his father and mother*** *and is joined to his wife*" (Mark 10:7). I pray for you and your family to experience God's plan. It works and saves you from a lot of grief and all the consequences that come from multiple partners. Recently I found encouragement when I read that more and more young people are choosing this for their lives. I think after watching the world and seeing its brokenness, they have concluded there is a better way. It is a great choice.

For many, the path to marriage includes some detours and disasters. I think about half of those I know have some sort of brokenness. The most common brokenness is tied to alcohol and drug abuse. The person they married becomes someone else. Sometimes those detours include secret abuse. Secrets have power over you as long as they are kept secret. When you bring them in the light, they lose their power. Your brokenness needs healing that comes from our Savior. The great thing about God is that it is never too late to start over. I encourage you to find trustworthy counselors to help you begin again and discover what God intended for you to experience in your marriage.

For some of you, your detours put you in many beds and you have lost the sacredness of sex. Promiscuity never gives us the kind of connection God intended for sex. Some experience same sex attraction. This is encouraged in our culture today. God's idea for sex was simple: one man for one woman with a commitment for life. If you are among the many who have experienced the broken world of sex, God has a solution for you. Push the restart button and allow God to cleanse you of your past and give you a fresh start. If you are living with deep secrets that have power over you, do not be ashamed anymore. If you have a habit that owns you, you will need confidential accountability.

For those of you who are married, get educated. Begin to understand sex and how you can fulfill each other. Sex was not designed to be a selfish thing. It is best expressed when focused on your partner and what fulfills them. If you approach sex with the idea of getting what you can out of it, you will be disappointed. The best part of sex is in the fulfillment of each other.

Audrey and I have learned to make sex a part of our adventure. In our younger days, my needs were far greater than Audrey's. There was a time when I had to explain to her how men work and how to help me with temptation by fulfilling my needs. This was an important conversation that was hard for me to talk about and hard for her to hear. The older we get, the more balanced the needs of each other are. We have learned to find ways to fulfill each other and stay focused on each other. Audrey points out that people should never stop learning and keep working on communicating with each other throughout their marriage. It is imperative in all areas of marriage, but especially in this area. We know that a satisfying sex life keeps temptation at bay. We have found a monthly conversation about sex helps us to keep discovering the adventure in our sex life.

Warning! There is a multi-billion dollar industry today that is robbing us of healthy sex lives. According to Tech Mission's website, about 70% of men and 28% of women struggle with pornography. The images now come right to our phones. The problem with this industry is the way it reduces people to objects. There is no relationship required there. Sex is reduced to an act and not a relationship. It is very addictive and robs many of the healthy relationship God intended for them. As long as this is a secret, it will hold power in your life. If you struggle here, you need to find someone to be honest with and accountable to. Good software can help reduce the temptation as well.

If more Christians took the time to bring adventure into their sex lives, there would be a lot less divorce and brokenness. If Abraham can have sex at 100, then you can develop your sex life at your age.

Chapter 10

Why Does God Give Us Teenagers?

I convinced Audrey, my daughter Kristen, and her boyfriend to go on a hike with me. I wanted it to be challenging for Kristen's boyfriend, but not so hard that I would be in trouble with my wife and my daughter. So I picked a fairly flat hike to get us to our campsite. The second day would have a challenging hike to a lake and I could test the metal of this guy, who was sixteen years old. We packed our gear and started to our campsite late in the day. Things went well for a while, but as the darkness was closing in I realized that I had miscalculated how long it would take us to get to our campsite. There were some in our party who were even questioning the existence of the campsite and my ability to navigate us to it. Some suggested that I was lost and that my skills as a leader were not up to par. There was definite talk of a mutiny when we found ourselves literally running in the dim light in hopes of making camp before dark. This was not the trip I had hoped for.

I cannot imagine the trip God had planned for Abraham to test his faith. After having enough faith to believe God would give him a child, he now would have his faith tested as never before.

> *Sometime later, God tested Abraham's faith. "Abraham!" God called. "Yes," he replied. "Here I am." "Take your son, your only son—yes, Isaac, whom*

you love so much—and go to the land of Moriah. Go and sacrifice him as a burnt offering on one of the mountains, which I will show you." (Genesis 22:1-2)

Faith is not what you *know*, it is what you *do*. Abraham had enough faith to simply obey - even if this was an impossible request.

The next morning, Abraham got up early. He saddled his donkey and took two of his servants with him, along with his son, Isaac. Then he chopped wood for a fire for a burnt offering and set out for the place God had told him about. On the third day of their journey, Abraham looked up and saw the place in the distance. "Stay here with the donkey," Abraham told the servants. "The boy and I will travel a little farther. We will worship there, and then we will come right back." (Genesis 22:3-5)

Faith is believing in the future. Hebrews 11:19 says that Abraham believed God would raise Isaac from the dead. He never lost faith that God would bring them both back to camp. Notice the word "we". The miracle he expected and believed would happen was not the same as what God had planned. God showed up in a different way. It was a different miracle that would save his boy.

And Abraham picked up the knife to kill his son as a sacrifice. At that moment the angel of the LORD called to him from heaven, "Abraham! Abraham!" "Yes," Abraham replied. "Here I am! Don't lay a hand on the boy!" the angel said. "Do not hurt him in any way, for now I know that you truly fear God. You have not withheld from Me even your son, your only son." (Genesis 22:10-12)

This not only tested Abraham, but it tested Isaac too. I cannot imagine what this young man thought of his test. I do know that this showed him how much faith his dad had in God. We need some kind of test that helps our kids too.

The Jewish faith and most other religions have some kind of rite of passage into adulthood. On one of our African adventures we met some young Masai boys. They were on their test. When a boy turns twelve in their culture, each family sends their boys out to live together and survive on their own. After one year they can come home again and they are accepted as an adult. This seems brilliant to me. People in their culture expect it and everyone helps the boys live their lives outside their homes. They become men. It is probably too dangerous for the United States, but we need something for our youth. You see, the journey changes the boys and the parents are forced to look at their children differently. Audrey and I found value in this, so when our son and daughter became a teenager, we decided to give them a test that prepared them for adulthood.

We read up on some of the different customs. Each custom had one thing in common: there was something hard that the child had to do or agree to do. We wanted to make our test difficult, so we included six days of testing, each with valuable life skills for our kids to be tested on. Every day would be a different value that we hoped they would develop as an adult.

Daniel was first up, so I began to think of a week-long test that would help prepare him for manhood. He was changing and I knew we had to change the way we disciplined and worked with him. It was obvious to us that he needed freedom and choices. He was showing signs of thinking on his own and blind obedience would not work anymore. I knew that he loved to hunt so the best motivator for him would be a gun. If he passed the week long test, I was prepared to give him the lever action Marlin 22 that my father had passed on to me. I decided to make it a six-day test that ended with a party. We planned a birthday party that was separate from the test. We also began to plan a party that would celebrate his passage. I assured him we would celebrate, but if he wanted this special gift he had to pass the test.

I never dreamed how meaningful the test would become. His rite of passage project was to spend a day in the wilderness on his own. I still cannot believe we did this. We left him at a little lake in the woods with all he needed to survive. He was fine, but we were worried sick. As the day passed, I began to think about the terrible things that could come from this ridiculous test. I was not sure he was really up for it. I saw him as a vulnerable child who could not survive. I wanted to protect him. I worried that the things he chose to bring along as he prepared for the day would not serve him well. It was a long day for us as parents.

When I went to pick him up, he was pumped! He had met a homeless family in the hills and befriended one of the boys. He knew the next thing on his test was to give away his favorite childhood toy. He asked me to retrieve his remote control car. It was expensive and soon I was regretting this part of the test. I watched him give the little boy his most prized possession. Tears rolled down my face as the boy could not believe his eyes. He dropped the car for a moment, ran into his tent and brought back a little compass. He handed it to Daniel and said "This is all I own. I want you to have it." We melted into tears and drove home talking about how blessed we were.

Daniel's Feedback as an Adult:

Turning thirteen was a moment most boys probably don't remember, but for me it was the moment when my father invited me to be a man. To do this, my father decided to have me stay out in the woods for an entire day by myself. This was so scary. I grew up watching movies like "Fire in the Sky" and "The Edge," so I was sure that death would come knocking at my door. I still remember my dad dropping me off at Beehive, twenty minutes out of Wenatchee, Washington with a fishing pole, pink and blue power bait, a raft and some dehydrated scalloped potatoes. When my father left I was all alone in the elements, so I started to bait my pole just like he had taught me, and I began to fish. There is nothing worse than being left alone in the woods - and yet there is nothing more adventurous to turn a boy into a man. I caught a fish and made a fire to cook it, all the while fearing the bears being drawn to me like flies. Time seemed to stand still and last forever. All I could do was think about fears and my family. Being alone was tough and, looking back, I see my dad was trying to show me that real men can handle tough stuff.

At about mid-day I noticed I wasn't the only one on the lake. A family who was homeless had hidden their tent just off the lake in the woods. Being alone drew me to their camp like a magnet, and a boy my age popped out. He came over to me and we talked for hours. He told me that his family had no home and that they lived on the lake eating fish and stuff that was given to them. As he talked, I noticed his clothes were torn and his hair was very tangled and dirty. I asked him if I could see where he was staying and he took me to his tent. His father was drinking and was probably drunk. His mother was sleeping and there was no question that this family was in the worst spot a family could be. The boy and I left their camp and went swimming and fishing. Before I knew it, darkness had set in and my dad pulled in to pick me up.

On the way home he told me that my next challenge was to give away my most prized possession to someone in need. I knew instantly this possession was my remote-controlled car and I knew it was this boy who would be the recipient. The next day we drove up to give away my best toy. I still remember the look on the boy's face as I returned to his home with such a great gift and just gave it away. My dad was trying to teach me that being a man was more than just going against fear. It was understanding that material possessions can be easily taken away from us, and yet we can be better for it. Adventures are all around.

I believe growing up in a family that's adventurous like ours is rare. From spearfishing in Nicaragua to hunting in Africa, my family experience has taught me to see life as an endless adventure. While many were growing up in church as kids being bored out of their minds, my father taught me that the church is the greatest adventure on earth, calling its people to lighten up and enjoy each other. We are called to do things new and wild, while drawing everyone out of their comfort zone. I also believe this has always been initiated with my father. The most adventure-minded man on earth reminding me that Jesus is found in the wide-open spaces of freedom and adventure. He teaches that the church is meant to invite the world into an awesome adventure.

Daniel finished all of his testing and received the Marlin 22.

Kristen came along and we had to adjust the testing a little. I was not leaving my girl in the woods alone all day! The rite of passage project I devised for her was to plan a meal and invite over her school principal. I did not believe that her principal would actually come; I just wanted Kristen to be bold. I wanted her to live life with confidence. The gift we had for her was her life-long dream of going to Disneyland. Kristen was very reluctant to do this part of the test. She put it off and completed every other part but this project. Each challenge became fun for her and she passed with flying colors. At the end of the week she decided that the potential teasing that would come from inviting the principal over was just too much. She left her project incomplete and did not go to Disneyland.

I found that this process was still a success for her. She wrote out her life plan and thought carefully about how she would live her life. She gained more than anyone from this test.

Kristen's Feedback as an Adult:

When I was young, I used to dread being told when it was my bedtime. Sometimes when I would complain, my parents would tell me that when I turned thirteen and could prove I was responsible, I would be able to choose my own bedtime. I longed for that day to come, and when it did, I was both

When my parents gave me the coming-of-age test, I remember sitting in my family room and starting to fill it out. I had a lot of my own questions regarding what each question meant. When I heard that my reward was Disneyland, I was beyond excited as it would be my first time there. I remember thinking that nothing would keep me from getting this prize. But as the realization set in for some of the challenges, I started to change my mind.
The first challenge in the test was to visit and help an older person in a nursing home by doing chores, reading, etc. I don't remember much about doing this actual challenge, but I do remember that this was not a scary test for me. I did not mind being around people in a nursing home and even as I have grown older, I still have a place in my heart for the elderly. The second challenge was to find an underprivileged girl and give away my prized possession. For this challenge, I remember giving away some very special stuffed animals to a young girl in our church. Later in life, my husband and I counseled a young couple for marriage and she told me that she was that same young girl.

I love that my gift ended up being a significant enough moment that she remembered and told me about it years later.

As I read the third challenge, this was where my struggle began. My parents had told me that I would have to make dinner for three sets of people. I had to pick out the recipe, go shop for the items, and cook the food all by myself. I was not surprised by this challenge as my mom was an amazing cook and she always tried to get me excited about cooking, but it never happened naturally. I do remember cooking a meal for my family and doing the shopping - I was so nervous about how it would turn out but my mom helped me a lot. The problem with this challenge was not so much making the food, but who I was to make it for. One of the sets of people was my principal or my vice principal of my Junior High School. Inviting my principal over for dinner and having her know me by name would have been social suicide. So, sadly enough, because I held my ground on not making dinner for my principal or vice principal and my parents held their ground on the challenge, I never won my trip to Disneyland.

As for the written part of the test, I really enjoyed looking back on my answers. In the Finding my Faith portion of the test, it was good to see that at the simplest form, I understood what it meant to be a Christian. My favorite answer was to the question "What is hell like?" to which I stated, "The worst place you can think of, I don't know because I haven't really been there, but it is horrible." In the Finding Friends portion, the questions were simple with good answers from me but one that stuck out was the question "What do you do with your enemies?" To which I stated, "See if there is a way to work things out, and improve on something they don't like." For a 13-year-old, being willing to improve on my faults is pretty neat to see; to remember to do that now, as I get older, would be great.

Considering that I was only thirteen, I am not sure where I was able to come up with the answers I did for the Finding a Spouse portion of the test. My guess is that my parents sat me down and talked to me before my test, or we had talks about sex and relationships in Junior High youth group. Regardless, I am very thankful today for the fact that I had to learn the answers to this test. At thirteen, I made a decision to be pure until I was married. I received a ring from my dad and stood in front of the entire church and made a promise. It was that promise with my dad and under God that allowed me to give the amazing gift of purity to my husband.

I also had to come up with one-year, five-year, and ten-year goals. For the one-year, they were all simple things like making the honor roll and singing in front of church. I did not achieve either of these goals. One reason being I just wasn't that interested in school and the other being I was too afraid that I would not sing well. For my five-year goals I had aspirations of raising money for college, which didn't happen because I used all my money to put towards a car when I turned sixteen. The only goals I actually achieved were my ten-year goals of graduating college and getting married. To some it might not seem valuable to ask a 13-year-old for goals for their future but because of this I have taken the concept of writing goals and carried it into my adult life. I have had goals in life for before having kids and professional goals that I am still working to achieve.

Even though I did not end up getting the big prize of going to Disneyland, I do remember finally getting to pick my own bedtime. After a few nights of staying up too late, I ended up going to bed early again just like my parents had me do. There was value for me even at a young age to learn natural consequences. Reflecting back on this test, I can see the value of encouraging children to address the issues they will soon see as adults. In fact, I would even add some challenges like watching a child for a full day or cleaning up the house for a full week. When my own children are old enough, I also plan to challenge them with a coming-of-age test. I just might choose to remove any challenge dealing with the principal or vice principal.

I, Dan, have created a generic rite of passage test based on what I gave Daniel and Kristen. You'll find it on page 65.

In the years that followed, we would be tested in different ways. One night Audrey and I were tested when there was rebellion in our family. After a couple of years of turmoil, my son walked out of the house in the middle of the night. He carried a change of clothes with him and announced he was not coming back. I was angry and Audrey was crying. This was not the family adventure we had planned on. I had always hoped my son would love life like I did. I had hoped that he would love God like I did. All of that was now in question. Our adventure was in shambles. What was next?

The reconciliation started with a meal together. He didn't want to come home, he just wanted to talk. He had found a place to live and needed some belongings from home. He spent most of his senior year living with another family. It was really a test of our faith. It was a time of great questioning. Who was I? Would I follow God even if my son didn't? What kind of example was I? Could I still lead my family and my church? I wanted to quit.

Then there was Audrey. She was angry too. She loved Daniel, but he had been controlling the household and our lives. He had been difficult to deal with when he was there, yet when he was gone there was always worry about what he was doing. Audrey had her own questions. How do you deal with the guilt of a mother's heart? How do you get beyond the anger and parent well? What was God's plan in this?

My hurt and brokenness became a vehicle for me to share with others. This test was a reminder that I was a wayward son too. I caused my Heavenly Father the same kind of grief. God's love for me never wavered. Could I have that kind of love for my son? I realized my pride and desire to have a family that was an example to everyone was gone. I quit giving advice and started listening. Those were days I will never forget. I learned that nobody had a secret plan that would bring a rebellious boy home.

One day Daniel returned home. Our son asked for our forgiveness. Now he leads his own church, Awaken in Wenatchee, Washington and speaks in our church. He loves God and life even more than I do. His relationship with Audrey and me has been restored. I learn from him all the time.

Teenagers test us. When we are in the midst of the test we must sacrifice, listen, and have faith that God will provide.

Chapter 11

Letting Go and Facing Our Humanity

I sat in a tiny house with a hole in the floor. It was not an outhouse, but it was the same size. The temperature was twenty below outside and eighty above on the inside. We had a fire and watched the open water below. Walter, Audrey's father, was teaching me to ice fish. We had a lead weighted, red-and-white fish dangling about six feet down in the 32° water. All of the sudden, a fish head the size of a shovel slid into view. I slowly steadied my small version of a devil's pitchfork with a rope tied to the end of it. We had placed the tip in the water in order to see the visual bend in the water caused by the diffused light. I carefully aimed my spear at a trophy northern, my first fish in Minnesota. I threw the spear and it sunk into the ground below. I missed. Walter laughed out loud at me. I missed quite a few times before I hit a fish that day. Walter said that if I put any more holes in the floor of the lake it would drain all the water out. This was my first trip home to meet Audrey's parents.

Walter was the best man you could have ever met. The best dad in the world! In my mind, I would have a hard time living up to that. He was loving, extremely generous, and treasured his time with his children. He was retired and 55 years old when Audrey was born. She spent a lot of time with him growing up. Some of her favorite memories include going to the doughnut shop, ice fishing, gardening and eating candy bars with him. The day I asked for

Audrey's hand in marriage he joked that I better take more than her hand. He never had much, but every time we went to visit he filled my gas tank and bought our breakfast. His kind heart was adored by anyone who took the time to get to know him.

He never once complained that I would take her away from him because of ministry. He loved God and was proud of Audrey and the work we were doing. He remained active until the age of 93 by working in the garden, riding a bike to town and helping every widow in his apartment complex. In just two short months, his health declined and he passed away.

Those final moments with Dad were memorable. But the one thing we took note of most was the love shown between Audrey's mom and her dad. We witnessed their last kiss as they said "So long, I will see you again."

I don't even want to think about when that time comes for Audrey and me. Selfishly, I want to go first. I don't think I can bear the pain. For Abraham, this had to have been tough.

> *When Sarah was 127 years old, she died at Kiriath-arba (now called Hebron) in the land of Canaan. There Abraham mourned and wept for her. (Genesis 23:1-2)*

You very rarely read in the Bible that someone wept. You hardly ever read a love story where the record of a death included a spouse that mourned.

> *Then Abraham buried his wife, Sarah, there in Canaan, in the cave of Machpelah, near Mamre (also called Hebron). So the field and the cave were transferred from the Hittites to Abraham for use as a permanent burial place. (Genesis 23:19-20)*

This is the end of the journey for them. Someday, every one of us will face this. Because of my profession I get to see the difference faith makes during this phase. For us, the journey's end is just a new beginning. There is a new heaven and a new earth. There is a place that is prepared for us. I don't think any of us can quite comprehend the next life, but it will be our faith in Jesus Christ that propels us there. Having faith that there is a future together helps us face the temporary separation from our loved ones.

When Audrey and I started dating we had a two-month period in which we did not see each other. I went to Bolivia to explore the possibility of working as a missionary there. On that long summer, Audrey and I could only communicate by mail. Our love grew deeper in separation. We longed for the day we would see each other again. I memorized her letters and wrote to her every day. Once in a while we would get the opportunity to talk over a ham radio. As the world listened in we would announce: "I love you. Over." The words were out there for all to hear over the radio waves. Those words gave me hope that we would soon be together.

I suspect that for those of you who have said "so long" to a loved one already, your longing will never end. But when one of us goes before the other, we have the promise found in a new adventure, one day exploring together again.

Let us not forget that for those of us who have put our faith in God "the best is yet to come." That is not just a saying, those are words I live my life by. I know that the future is always brighter than the past. So, when God calls you out to adventure with Him, take Him up on the offer. It is worth every step.

Rite of Passage Test

Some of these questions were used for a specific child and not both. It is up to each parent to make that decision for their own child. Please adapt this to your child's individuality and personality.

Directions for kids:
Read all the way through. You may ask for help but you must do this yourself.

Monday

I. Face the Facts – Survival
   a. Plan a camp out or entertaining meal, to be accomplished by the end of the week
      i. (Option 1) Plan a trip to camp out all night alone, find your way there and back.
         1. What is the budget?
         2. Where to go?
         3. What to eat?
         4. What to take?
         5. How to cook the food?
      ii. (Option 2) Plan a picnic or meal.
         1. What is the budget?
         2. Where to go or serve at home?
         3. Set time of day.

4. Who to invite? Send invites (parents, grandparents, friends).
5. Plan meal.
6. Purchase food.
7. Prepare food.
8. Plan serving, entertainment, music, etc.

b. How much money does it cost for our family to live for a month?
   i. Budget it out on a sheet of paper.
      1. Lodging
      2. Food
      3. Utilities
      4. Phone
      5. Car
      6. Gas
      7. Insurance
      8. Clothing
      9. Recreation
      10. Savings

c. Plan a budget for you to live on your own.

Tuesday

II. Finding My Faith

a. Where does real strength come from?
b. What do you believe about God?
c. Who is Jesus?
d. Can you earn your way to heaven?
e. What is hell like?

f. Do you believe in evolution or creation? Why?
g. How do you have a relationship with God?
h. How do you know God is real?
i. When is the last time God talked to you?
j. How do you listen to God?
k. Why should you pray?
l. How often should you read the Bible? Why?
m. How do you find a good church?
n. Why should you go to church?
o. How do you know you will make it to heaven?
p. List 3 questions that you have about God.

Wednesday

III. Finding Friends – Who is your neighbor?
a. What should you do to your enemies?
b. Do you always have to forgive? Why?
c. What does it mean to forgive?
d. How do you become a good friend?
e. What makes a bad friend?
f. How do you stop a bad friendship?
g. Project #1 – Visit and help an older person by doing chores, reading, etc. (find a needy senior citizen, person in a rest home, handicapped person, neighbor, or acquaintance).
h. Project #2 – Find an underprivileged boy/girl and give away a prized

possession. (check apartment complex, call a mission)

Thursday

IV. Finding a Spouse – Relationships with boys/girls

a. When can you date?
b. Complete this sentence with 10 different answers: "When on a date I should never…"
c. Complete this sentence with 10 different answers: "When on a date I should always…"
d. What should you look for in a wife/husband? (List 10 traits)
e. How will you know she/he is the right person to marry?
f. How do you know when to get married?
g. Why did God create sex?
h. Is sex good or bad?
i. How can you control the sex drive God put in you?
j. What does God allow in dating before you get married? (List 10 things)
k. What does God not allow before marriage and why?
l. If you become pregnant before marriage, is abortion an okay option?

Friday

V. Facing my Future (List everything that applies)
   a. What special desires and interests has God put in you?
   b. What do you enjoy doing?
   c. What do you do well?
   d. What do you think God wants you to do?
   e. Should you go to college?
   f. What should you study in college?
   g. Should you go to a specialty school? (carpentry, dentistry, plumbing, etc.)
   h. How will you pay for it?
   i. Write out 5 goals for yourself that are to be reached in each of the following time frames:
      i. One Year Goals – (grades, sports, church, etc.)
      ii. Five Year Goals
      iii. Ten Year Goals

VI. Celebrate Success – Are you an adult?
   a. Is a teenager an adult?
   b. What do adults do differently than children?
   c. List 5 things that makes a person mature.
   d. List 5 responsibilities you have now.
   e. List 5 freedoms you have now.
   f. Name a responsibility and a freedom that you wish to have.
   g. What special gift would you like for your birthday?

You will be given a
___________________________________ upon successful completion of this test. You may choose something different if you would like.

Study Guide

Chapter 1

Getting Started… Who was your first crush?

1. The message Dan received was clear: "No way!" We will all most likely face a "No way!" moment at some point in our lives (it may come as a response to a job interview, from a friend, from a love interest, etc.) How have you recovered from the "No ways" in your life?

2. There will always be someone who will count us out, or overlook us. Thankfully, our true value comes from above. 1 Peter 1:18-19 reads, "For you know that God paid a ransom to save you from the empty life you inherited from your ancestors. And the ransom he paid was not mere gold or silver. It was the precious blood of Christ, the sinless, spotless Lamb of God." The high value God attaches to our lives is seen in the high price he paid for us. What was the price?

3. "It is easy to stop halfway. It is easy to get weary. Have you found yourself on a journey that you want to stop? Read Isaiah 40:31, and make it your prayer. Ask God to give you new strength. "Those who trust in the Lord will find new strength. They will soar high on wings like eagles. They will run and not grow weary. They will walk and not faint."

"Success is not final; failure is not fatal: it is the courage to continue that counts." Winston Churchill

Supplemental reads: Mark #17: The Wisdom to Deal with Failure; bible.org, "A Prayer for when you feel like giving up" Rachelwojo.com, Aug. 16th, 2013.

Chapter 2

Getting Started… Who was your first date with, and where did you go?

1. Pastor Dan had originally planned on living his life on the mission field. When you were young, did you start out with one set of plans, and end up going in a completely different direction?

2. If you are married, were there requirements your spouse had to meet? Pastor Dan wanted someone who would adventure with him into the unknown. He wanted someone who could hunt. If you are not married, what are your non–negotiables?

3. "… only God can remove the ugliness of the human soul. Only God can create a new person." Ezekiel 36:26 says, "And I will give you a new heart, and I will put a new spirit in you. I will take out your stony, stubborn heart and give you a tender, responsive heart." Have you experienced God re-creating you in some fashion?

4. Are you ready to believe God's promise for your family?

Chapter 3

Getting Started… This chapter is called "Dream of Adventure." If money were not an issue, what adventure would you go on, or trip would you take?

1. The first hike Pastor Dan chose "stirred his soul." What stirs your soul? (Being by the water, music, teaching kids, sunsets, operating in your wheelhouse at work.)

2. Pastor Dan said, "The more hard things I do, the easier life seems to me." Sometimes God asks us to follow Him through hard places, too. Is there a hard place that God has asked you to follow Him through?

3. Where is God calling you? Often, to follow God, we have to let go of what is comfortable and familiar. What do you have to let go of or leave behind?

4. What dream does God have for you to hang on to?

5. What steps have you taken or not taken toward that dream?

Chapter 4

Getting Started… "One thing I noticed very quickly, no matter how fast you run, you will never catch a caribou." In your hobbies, or pursuits, what humorous lessons have you learned?

1. Sometimes until we look back, we don't realize we are leaving people behind us for relationships, work, etc. Have you caught yourself doing this before?

2. "Our culture begs us to sell ourselves for the attraction of the outside." Read 1 Samuel 16:7 "…The Lord doesn't see things the way you see them. People judge by outward appearance, but the Lord looks at the heart." Have you ever judged a "book" by its cover, and discovered that you were completely mistaken?

3. What are you doing to protect your family from pornography?

4. Every year for the last several years, Pastor Dan has invited the congregation to read the

One Year Bible along with the staff. He refers to the Bible as "soap for the mind". If you are not reading the One Year, do you have another routine in place to keep your mind renewed?

*You can read or listen to the One Year Bible, and find lots of other great reading plans all by downloading YouVersion, a free Bible app.

Chapter 5

Getting Started... Pastor Dan & Audrey found themselves in Guatemala one December. Where's the farthest destination you've traveled to?

1. Pastor Dan stated in Chapter 2, "In the early days of ministry we learned that God takes care of those who generously give." Philippians 4:19 says, "You can be sure that God will take care of everything you need, his generosity exceeding even yours in the glory that pours from Jesus." (The MSG) Have you experienced God's generosity in your life?

2. Psalm 37:23-24 says, "The Lord directs the steps of the godly. He delights in every detail of their lives. Though they stumble, they will never fall, for the LORD holds them by the hand." Those of you that tithe, have you seen God bless you in spite of financial mis-steps?

3. The decision to tithe involves obedience. "Obedience to God's spirit is sometimes counter to our checkbook." Have you experienced this in your life? (For example, has God called you to take a trip that you didn't know how you were going to pay for, or have you felt like He has wanted you to give when you didn't think you had the funds?)

4. "That was a defining moment for Abraham. His act of humility and generosity moved him away from Sodom and Gomorrah. It brought him to a new level of faith." What in your life has brought you to a new level of faith? (For some of you maybe it's attending church for the first time, getting into a Connect group, etc.)

Chapter 6

Getting Started... Chapter 6 opens with the physical challenges of climbing Kilimanjaro. What is the most physically challenging thing you have ever done?

1. Read Psalm 11:4, Psalm 14: 2, and Psalm 33:13-14. What is the common theme of these verses?

2. Pastor Dan was persistent and determined in pressing on during his climb, and that was the only way he made it to the summit. Abraham was persistent in his belief. Has there been a time where the going was tough, and you had to just persist?

3. Romans 4:18-24 is an awesome summary of Abraham's faith, the reality of what he was up against, and 5 ideas that can be used as a model for us. Read this in the NIV, and list out the 5 ideals that Abraham held fast to.

For reference…

- Against all hope, Abraham in hope believed
- Without weakening in his faith, he faced the facts (Sarah's body was as good as dead)
- He did not waver through unbelief regarding God's promise
- He was strengthened in his faith, and gave glory to God
- He was fully persuaded that God had the power to do what he had promised

4. What is your next step?

Chapter 7

Getting Started… Thanks to some old sleds, the Kelloggs learned they loved to snowmobile. Does your family have a favorite way to spend free time? (on the water, watching movies, hiking, etc.)

1. "My passion was waning because I had lost my purpose. I lost the vision God gave me and my balance in life." Has there been a

point in your life where you could relate to these statements?

2. Have you ever taken a sabbatical from a job or a project, and had a hard time returning, but knew you were supposed to?

3. "Each trip into the wilderness began to restore my soul and my health." What do you do that restores your soul?

Chapter 8

Getting Started... Pastor Dan & Audrey unintentionally became the distraction at the watering hole. What's your best story about laughing when it was completely inappropriate (weddings, somber occasions, etc.)?

1. "When God asks you to believe in the impossible, laugh at how much you need God to come through for you." What do you need to laugh at right now?

2. Sometimes what appears to be an imposition (like adding two unplanned passengers) can turn out to be a blessing. How have you experienced this in your life?

3. "When you are on His adventure you can be sure He is watching over you and will help you." Is there a time you can look back on where you know God was watching over you and came to the rescue?

Chapter 9

Getting Started… The Himba tribe never bathes, except in smoke. What's the longest you have ever had to rough it (gone without a shower, etc.)?

1. Who taught you about sex?

2. "The LORD kept His word and did for Sarah exactly what He had promised." Is there a promise that you are still waiting to see fulfilled?

3. Is there a Christian book you have read to educate yourself in a healthy way about sex that you would recommend to others?

4. Lamentations 3:20-23 says, "I will never forget this awful time, as I grieve over my loss. Yet I still dare to hope when I remember this: The faithful love of the Lord never ends! His mercies never cease. Great is his faithfulness; his mercies begin afresh each morning." Is there an area that you need to "dare to hope for"?

5. What action do you need to take? (Have a conversation with a child, read a book, find an accountability partner, etc.)

A prayer about starting over:
Lord, when the past overtakes us, and the future overwhelms us, help us to cast our cares on You. Grant us new life and fresh grace to begin again. Mend relationships, heal wounds that fester, and give us persistence to press on toward the goal You have set for us. Put heaven in our eyes and eternity on our minds. Thank you for new beginnings. http://www.rebeccabarlowjordan.com/is-starting-over-possible/

Chapter 10

Getting Started… What kind of 12 year old were you?

1. "Faith is not what you *know*, it is what you *do*." Do you agree with that statement?

2. The miracle Abraham was expecting did not happen. God showed up in a different way. Have you experienced this? You were watching for God to do something one way, but He worked in a different way.

3. What are you afraid of with your kids?

4. What test will you give?

Chapter 11

Getting Started… When is the last time you tried something new you have never done before (like ice fishing)?

1. Have you ever been separated from those you love for an extended period of time?

2. Audrey's father was known to have a kind heart. He lived a long life, and lived it well. Have you had the privilege of knowing someone like that?

3. Is there someone you have said "so long" to already that you can't wait to see on the other side?

4. If you could live to be 127-years-old like Sarah, what would you hope to accomplish?